My Times Pocket Book

Oma Adigwe

Pupils who have mastered their times tables, gain a solid foundation in mathematics that will help them throughout secondary school and beyond.

1 x 1 = 1

2 x 1 = 2

3 x 1 = 3

4 x 1 = 4

5 x 1 = 5

6 x 1 = 6

7 x 1 = 7

8 x 1 = 8

9 x 1 = 9

10 x 1 = 10

11 x 1 = 11

12 x 1 = 12

1 x 2 = 2
2 x 2 = 4
3 x 2 = 6
4 x 2 = 8
5 x 2 = 10
6 x 2 = 12
7 x 2 = 14
8 x 2 = 16
9 x 2 = 18
10 x 2 = 20
11 x 2 = 22
12 x 2 = 24

1 x 3= 3

2 x 3 = 6

3 x 3 = 9

4 x 3 = 12

5 x 3 = 15

6 x 3 = 18

7 x 3 = 21

8 x 3 = 24

9 x 3 = 27

10 x 3 = 30

11 x 3 = 33

12 x 3 = 36

1 x 4 = 4

2 x 4 = 8

3 x 4 = 12

4 x 4 = 16

5 x 4 = 20

6 x 4 = 24

7 x 4 = 28

8 x 4 = 32

9 x 4 = 36

10 x 4 = 40

11 x 4 = 44

12 x 4 = 48

1 x 5 = 5
2 x 5 = 10
3 x 5 = 15
4 x 5 = 20
5 x 5 = 25
6 x 5 = 30
7 x 5 = 35
8 x 5 = 40
9 x 5 = 45
10 x 5 = 50
11 x 5 = 55
12 x 5 = 60

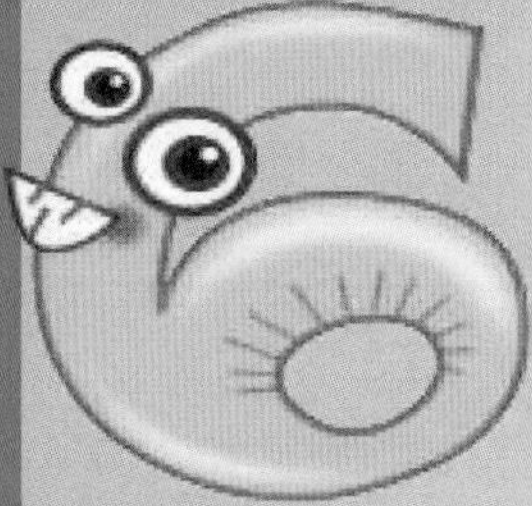

1 x 6 = 6
2 x 6 = 12
3 x 6 = 18
4 x 6 = 24
5 x 6 = 30
6 x 6 = 36
7 x 6 = 42
8 x 6 = 48
9 x 6 = 54
10 x 6 = 60
11 x 6 = 66
12 x 6 = 72

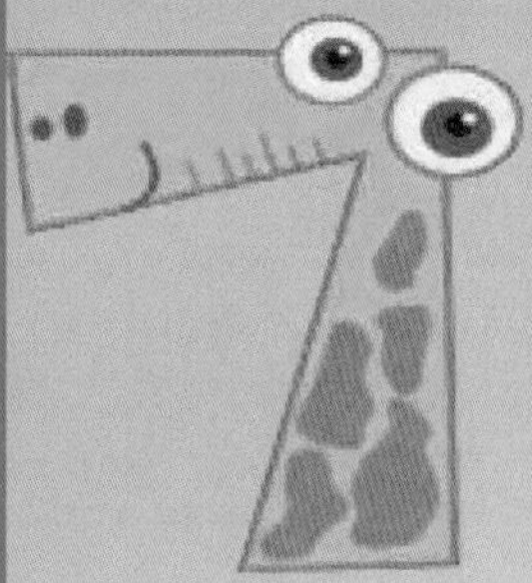

1 x 7 = 7

2 x 7 = 14

3 x 7 = 21

4 x 7 = 28

5 x 7 = 35

6 x 7 = 42

7 x 7 = 49

8 x 7 = 56

9 x 7 = 63

10 x 7 = 70

11 x 7 = 77

12 x 7 = 84

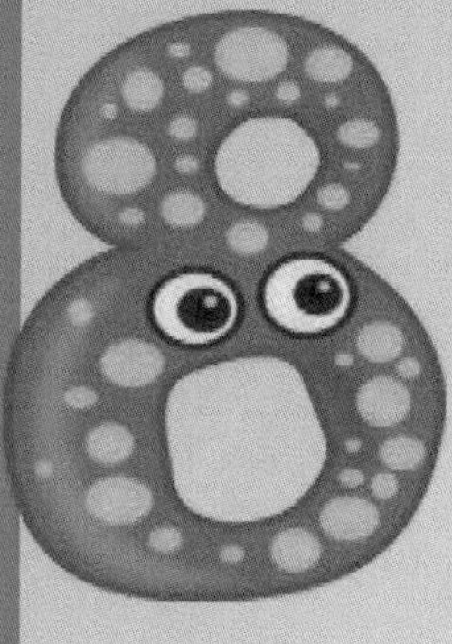

1 x 8 = 8

2 x 8 = 16

3 x 8 = 24

4 x 8 = 32

5 x 8 = 40

6 x 8 = 48

7 x 8 = 56

8 x 8 = 64

9 x 8 = 72

10 x 8 = 80

11 x 8 = 88

12 x 8 = 96

1 x 9 = 9

2 x 9 = 18

3 x 9 = 27

4 x 9 = 36

5 x 9 = 45

6 x 9 = 54

7 x 9 = 63

8 x 9 = 72

9 x 9 = 81

10 x 9 = 90

11 x 9 = 99

12 x 9 = 108

1 x 10 = 10
2 x 10 = 20
3 x 10 = 30
4 x 10 = 40
5 x 10 = 50
6 x 10 = 60
7 x 10 = 70
8 x 10 = 80
9 x 10 = 90
10 x 10 = 100
11 x 10 = 110
12 x 10 = 120

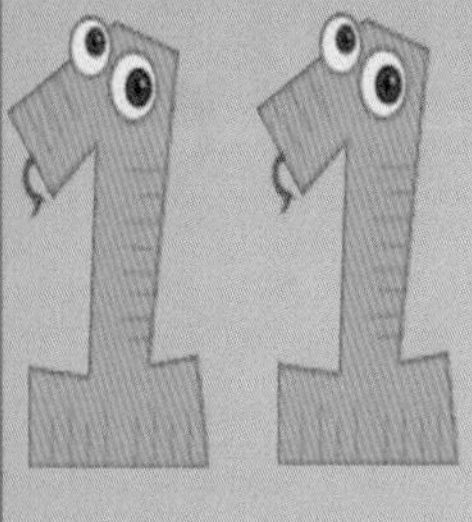

1 x 11 = 11

2 x 11 = 22

3 x 11 = 33

4 x 11 = 44

5 x 11 = 55

6 x 11 = 66

7 x 11 = 77

8 x 11 = 88

9 x 11 = 99

10 x 11= 110

11 x 11 = 121

12 x 11 = 132

1 x 12 = 12

2 x 12 = 24

3 x 12 = 36

4 x 12 = 48

5 x 12 = 60

6 x 12 = 72

7 x 12 = 84

8 x 12 = 96

9 x 12 = 108

10 x 12 = 120

11 x 12 = 132

12 x 12 = 144

	1	2	3	4	5	6	7	8	9	10	11	12
1	1	2	3	4	5	6	7	8	9	10	11	12
2	2	4	6	8	10	12	14	16	18	20	22	24
3	3	6	9	12	15	18	21	24	27	30	33	36
4	4	8	12	16	20	24	28	32	36	40	44	48
5	5	10	15	20	25	30	35	40	45	50	55	60
6	6	12	18	24	30	36	42	48	54	60	66	72
7	7	14	21	28	35	42	49	56	63	70	77	84
8	8	16	24	32	40	48	56	64	72	80	88	96
9	9	18	27	36	45	54	63	72	81	90	99	108
10	10	20	30	40	50	60	70	80	90	100	110	120
11	11	22	33	44	55	66	77	88	99	110	121	132
12	12	24	36	48	60	72	84	96	108	120	132	144

x	0	1	2	3	4	5	6	7	8	9	10	11	12
0													
1													
2													
3													
4													
5													
6													
7													
8													
9													
10													
11													
12													

X	0	1	2	3	4	5	6	7	8	9	10	11	12
0													
1													
2													
3													
4													
5													
6													
7													
8													
9													
10													
11													
12													

X	0	1	2	3	4	5	6	7	8	9	10	11	12
0													
1													
2													
3													
4													
5													
6													
7													
8													
9													
10													
11													
12													

X	0	1	2	3	4	5	6	7	8	9	10	11	12
0													
1													
2													
3													
4													
5													
6													
7													
8													
9													
10													
11													
12													

X	0	1	2	3	4	5	6	7	8	9	10	11	12
0													
1													
2													
3													
4													
5													
6													
7													
8													
9													
10													
11													
12													

x	0	1	2	3	4	5	6	7	8	9	10	11	12
0													
1													
2													
3													
4													
5													
6													
7													
8													
9													
10													
11													
12													

X	0	1	2	3	4	5	6	7	8	9	10	11	12
0													
1													
2													
3													
4													
5													
6													
7													
8													
9													
10													
11													
12													

Times tables mastery comes by constant practice and children who practice their times tables daily find it easier to develop that mastery thereby grasping the key concepts and building blocks of mathematics.

Printed in Great Britain
by Amazon

66983442R00015